Cover Art: **Railroad Pier,** 2014, 18" x 24" oil on canvas

Gregory Frux
Brooklyn Plein Air
June 2018

Arts & Adventures Publications with the
Tabla Rasa Gallery, 224 48 Street Brooklyn, NY 11220

4

Education of a Realist Painter in Brooklyn
by Gregory William Frux

My life changed one year when I was young teen. A trip to New York's Metropolitan Museum of Art brought me face to face with a special show of 19th Century French (Academic) painters. I was stunned to see what it was possible to do with oil paint on canvas— the power and intensity of artists like David, Ingres and Delacroix. I wanted to learn these skills.

Surely, I thought, these are lost arts; no one paints like this now. I remember the bright shock of the first time I saw artist Harvey Dinnerstein's paintings reproduced in a magazine. Here was a painter, apparently living, using classical tools to tell contemporary stories. What was more, he lived in Brooklyn, not more than two miles from my home, and he took on students.

I gradually discovered that there was cabal of realist artists, many living within walking distance of me in... Brooklyn! Realism was, in that era, the 1970s, profoundly unfashionable. Yet a few artists continued to plug away, using these tools to communicate what was in their hearts.

Where I grew up turned out to be a remarkably rich and inspiring place to study art. Access to the greatest master painters was a subway ride away. Prospect Park's landscape architecture and the 19th Century brownstone ornament evoked powerful mythic associations. Living artists carried on various aesthetic traditions, including a veteran of the Harlem Renaissance, Ernest Critchlow, who was my first teacher. Later, my parents were smart and perceptive enough to enroll me at the Brooklyn Museum Art School. It was, at the time, a vibrant hub for the visual arts.

I began studies with the painter Andy Reiss, an intense, sometimes difficult man, deeply engaged in academic teaching of art. After my time at the museum I shifted to private studies at his Park Slope apartment on Garfield Place. His cluttered home was filled with art books, plaster casts, jazz records, bedding, old chairs, half-finished paintings and sketches, and it smelled of marijuana. For a budding teenager, it was an incredibly evocative suggestion of what an artist's life could look like.

Andy told me that studying to be an artist was as demanding as becoming a doctor and took the same amount of time—seven years. He introduced me to modern realist painters, especially Edward Hopper. I continued to work with Andy throughout my high school years. After completing my time with him, he suggested a program of study to follow and two teachers to study with. Those teachers were Harvey Dinnerstein at the National Academy of Design and Lennart Anderson at Brooklyn College. I faithfully followed his plan, which eventually took more than a decade.

While my parents supported art studies, they didn't believe a career as an artist was viable. I studied architecture at City College of New York, emerging with a Bachelor of Architecture in 1981 and gaining my professional license three year later. I got a great job with New York City government designing and upgrading school buildings for the Board of Education. Later, in the 1990s, I became a curator the Board's art collection of 1400 murals, paintings and sculptures.

At the same time I was determined to pursue my studies and be an artist. Somehow, during my senior year of architecture school I managed to take classes with Harvey Dinnerstein, painting five mornings a week. It was an intense and illuminating class, working from a live model, in the same pose over a two week period. I am grateful to have had a year of Harvey's sensitive and thoughtful instruction.

When I began full time work, painting was confined to evenings and weekends. Yet within two years I was enrolled for Master of Fine Arts studies at Brooklyn College-- classes were in the later afternoon and evening and I was able to go part time while continuing to work. My teacher and thesis advisor was Lennart Anderson, an extremely perceptive painter and sensitive teacher. He taught me a great deal about how to render light in oil paints. Using the simplest of means, doing one still life painting each three hour studio class, he taught me profound observational skills. And when I graduated, I had completed my formal studies and was ready to use my knowledge to tell my stories.

While at Brooklyn College I took 3 courses studying overseas in Italy. There I gained the confidence and tools to paint outdoors in the marble town of Carrara. Returning to New York, I began to work on the streets, creating cityscapes of the East Village and Lower East Side. These canvases often told stories using 19th Century buildings and later additions. The old stories, waves of immigrants and remains of radical life were all threads in in these paintings. I was inspired by Edward Hopper's ways of dramatizing the city and his works where the presence of humans was implicit, rather than overt.

In 1992 I moved back to Park Slope in Brooklyn, at the edge of a landmark district. I connected strongly with the carved brownstones and architecture of Prospect Park. The landscape feels to me a mix of mythic and workaday. My paintings explore the history, but also the unique lighting effects of brownstone Brooklyn. I also celebrate a neighborhood which is a safe and comfortable home to tens of thousands. I hope to celebrate the civility and endurance of this comfortable way of life— with paintings of row houses, street trees, historic buildings and welcoming stoops.

In the last decade, people began showing up in the paintings. At first they appeared to serve a sense of scale, but they are also representing our community. Showing the diversity of Brooklyn felt important, the rich mix of people who share this special place. Several paintings have multiple characters and the stories begin to emerge— a woman with a roller suitcase looking over her shoulder, a couple loading a heavy duffle before a departure, a worried man looking skyward and others looking beyond our vantage point. Instead of illustrating a particular narratives, the character inhabiting the works offer a point of entry into this world.

Art as Ecotone
by Rowland S. Russell, PhD

For over 40 years I've been inspired and illuminated by Greg's art. Moreover, I have been significantly informed by our engaging and creative friendship. When we first met in the dorms at State University of New York at Binghamton in 1976, I had no idea how deeply our lives would intertwine. Though we only intersected there for one year before Greg moved back to New York City to complete his studies, our connection carried over through many passages and across many locales.

Over the years, Greg and I have explored together a diverse range of landscapes, including the White Mountains of New Hampshire, Strathcona Park in British Columbia, Seattle and the Olympic Peninsula in Washington State, Joshua Tree National Park in California, Northern New Mexico, West Texas and Eastern Oregon often accompanied by his wife, the painter Janet Morgan. On every excursion, Greg made art, sketching in his journal, setting up to paint a scene. I really got to witness his practice as a "plein air" artist when I was privileged to join Greg and Janet on two separate artists-in-residences at Death Valley National park as a guest writer.

But the landscapes I have shared most deeply with Greg have been the wilds of New York City. When I relocated back east from a dozen years living in Washington State, my Western friends commiserated with me over longing for the many wilderness areas I had grown to love out there. "When I really miss wilderness" I joked, "I'll head to the last true wilderness on the East Coast – New York!" Noted author Barry Lopez once told me that if one wanted to truly learn about ecology, they should spend time in New York City. Over countless long walks and city-scape explorations, Greg and I have explored these notions of urban wilderness and city ecology, as artists and as naturalists, both of which draw deeply on close attention to detail and recognition of nuance, and benefit from constant practice and meticulous research.

Whether he's portraying quiet scenes from Brooklyn's Prospect Park or the Botanical Gardens, intriguing remnants of New York's varied industry (grain silos, cement plants, cranes, piers), large or small scale architectural details (bridges, buildings, brownstone stoops), poignant scenes from the neighborhood or engaging vignettes of people enjoying the city, Greg's paintings invariably carry meticulous details that resonate deeply on emotional, philosophical and political planes.

In natural history, an ecotone is a place where different plant and animal communities overlap. Such a zone is inclusive of organisms from each region, but gives rise to diverse life forms that are not found in either separate place. In ecology, an ecotone is characterized by unique and unexpected qualities of life. For me, Greg's life and art function as a creative ecotone; offering a unique vision that incorporates the depth of human experience of urban architecture, history and culture as well as wild and elemental nature, with vitality not present in either genre apart from the other. There is also a kind of ecotone that exists between our inner selves and outer worlds. Greg's work speaks eloquently to the complex relationships people have with their places; figures in his paintings are telling us stories if we have eyes to discern them.

As a writer of natural history and scholar of 'sense of place' literature, I feel Greg's paintings - both urban and wilderness subjects - evoke a unique and deeply felt sense of the human experience of place. In both his life and his art, Greg transcends the dichotomies between city and wild places. He is able to draw from one to sustain and inform the other, resulting in a deeper experience of both. It is art which celebrates paradox; embracing apparently contradictory themes without needing to resolve the tension between them.

I fear the rift of values between wilderness and urban places is one which potentially threatens the fabric of society. A number of his paintings are set along waterfront that due to the potential impact of climate change and rising sea levels may not be present a generation from now if we are not able to transform our extractive relationship with the planet that sustains us into a more collaborative one. Greg's accurate and impassioned work in each realm transcends the divide that isolates us from the places that sustain us. His art shows us that love and respect for beauty in place is to be celebrated wherever we are.

Rowland S. Russell, PhD

Rowland has combined writing, art, music, teaching, mentoring and consulting into a multifaceted career. In his studies in natural history and ecology, he's found the inspiration and wisdom that informs his creative process, professional practice, and spiritual discipline.

Halloween, 1995, 24" x 36" oil on plywood

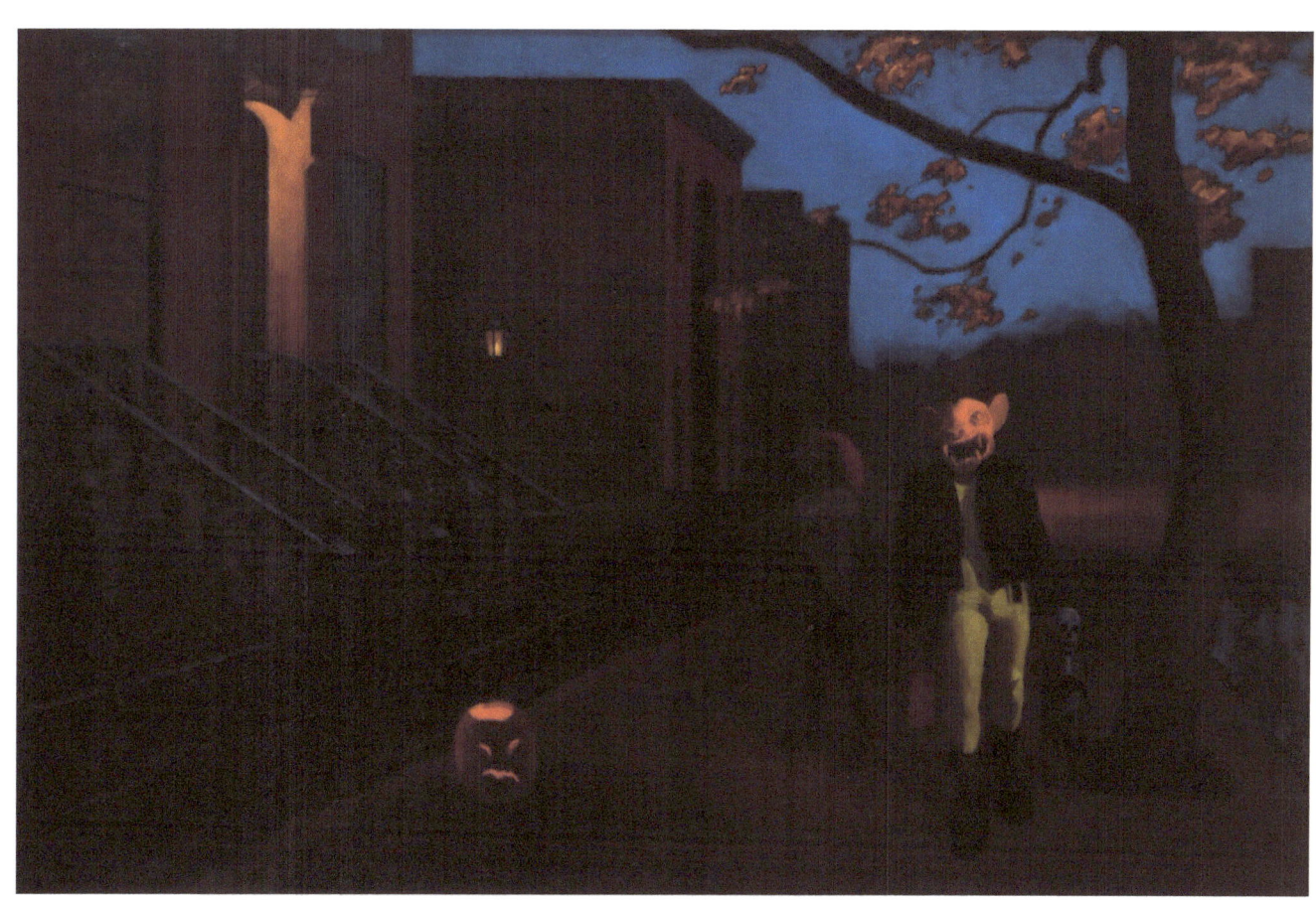

Gowanus Silos, 1996, 12" x 16" oil on canvas

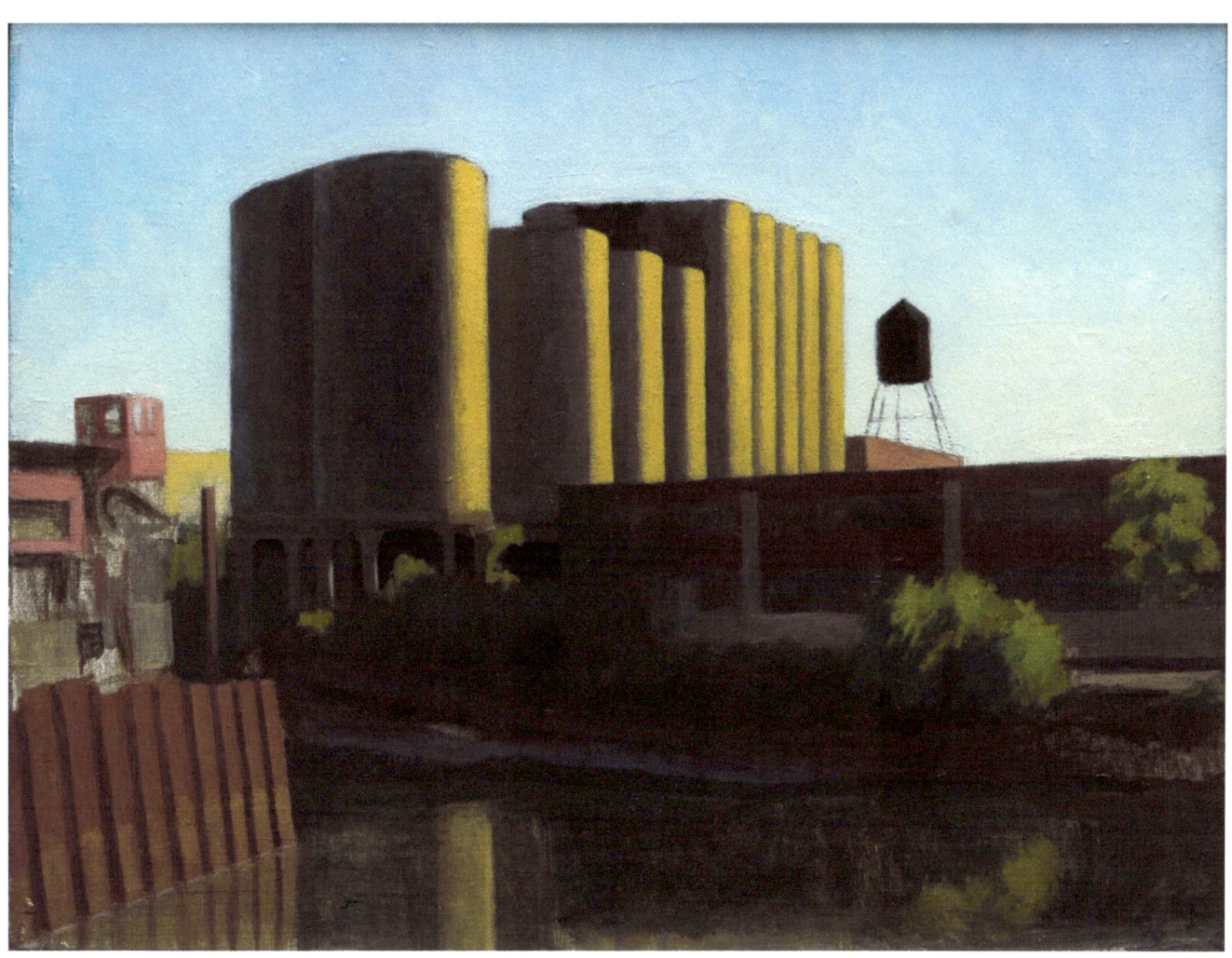

Steel Tower, 2000, 20" x 10" oil on canvas

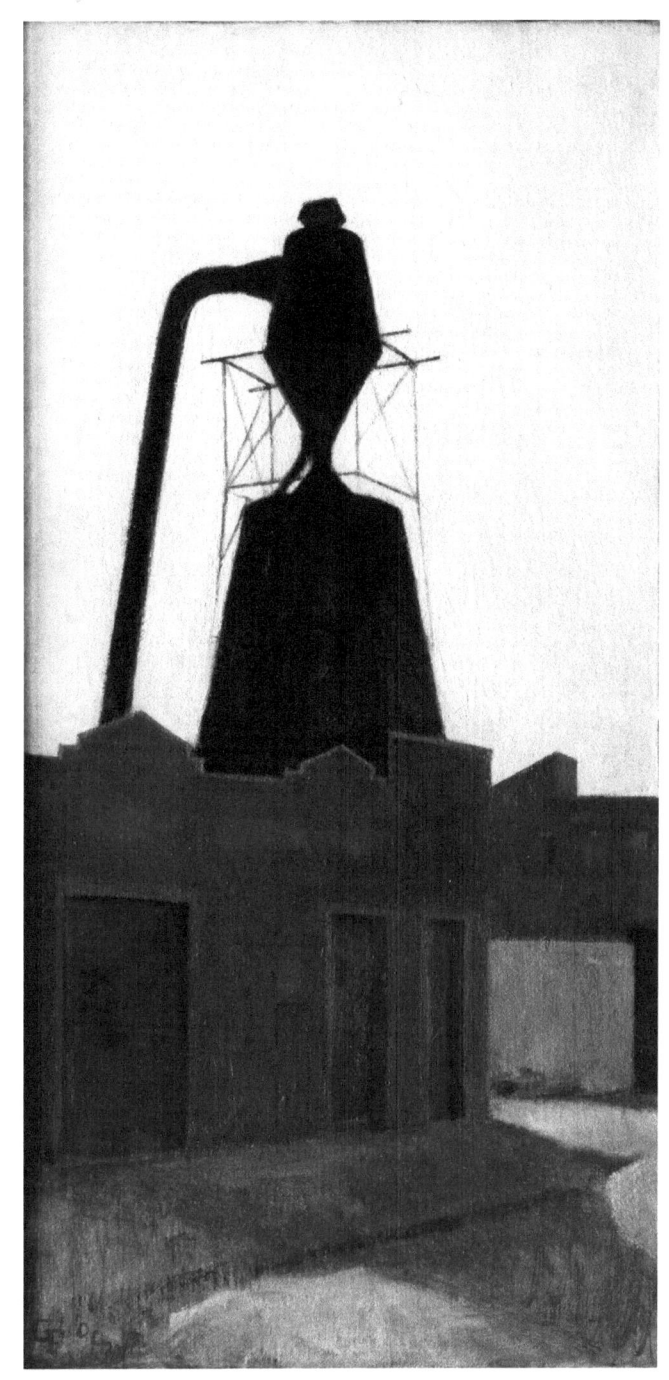

Elvis on Stoop, 2001, 17" x 25 1/2" oil on plywood

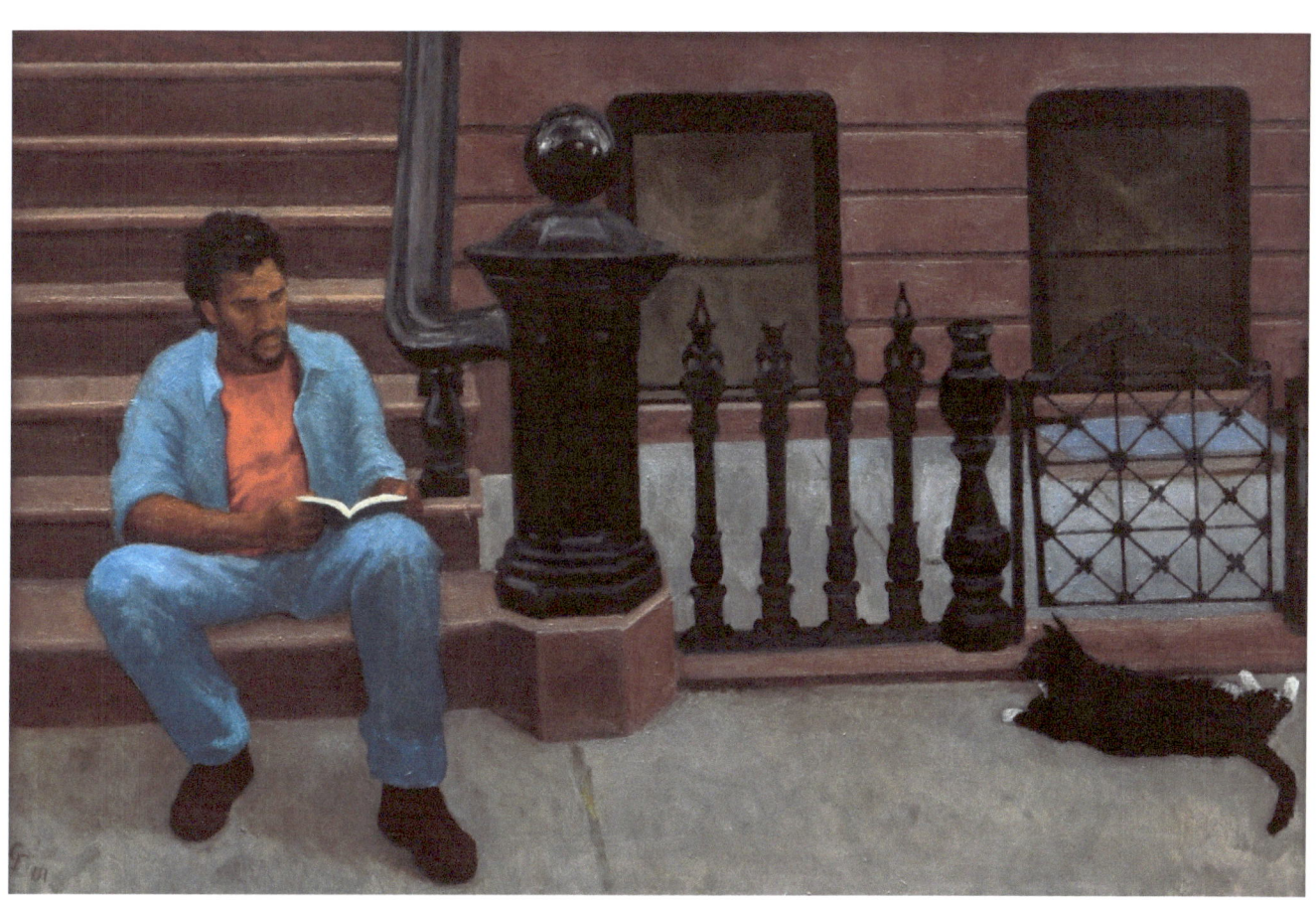

Union Street Firestation, 2002, 24" x 18" oil on canvas

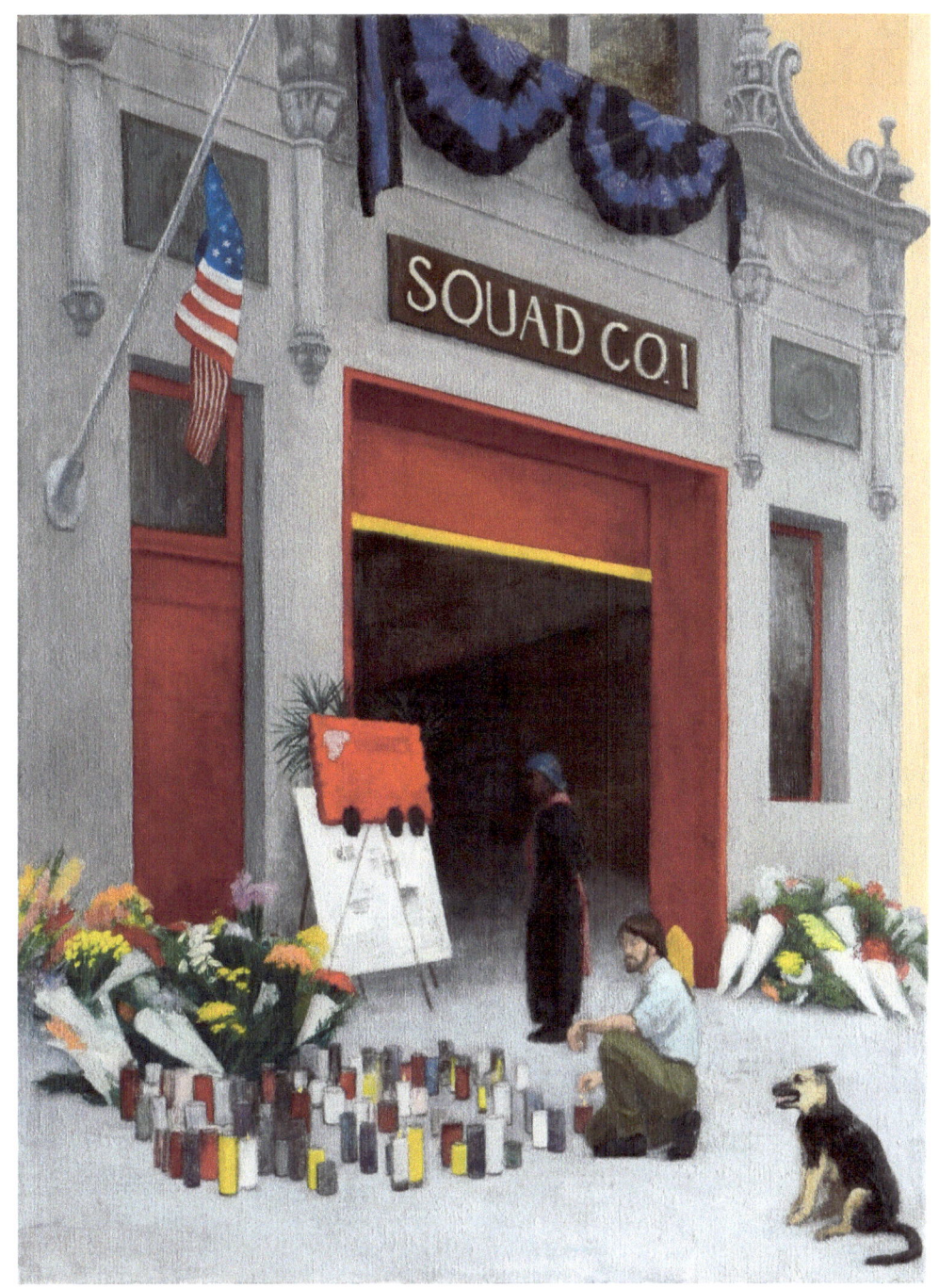

Cement Tower, 2002, 20" x 10" oil on canvas

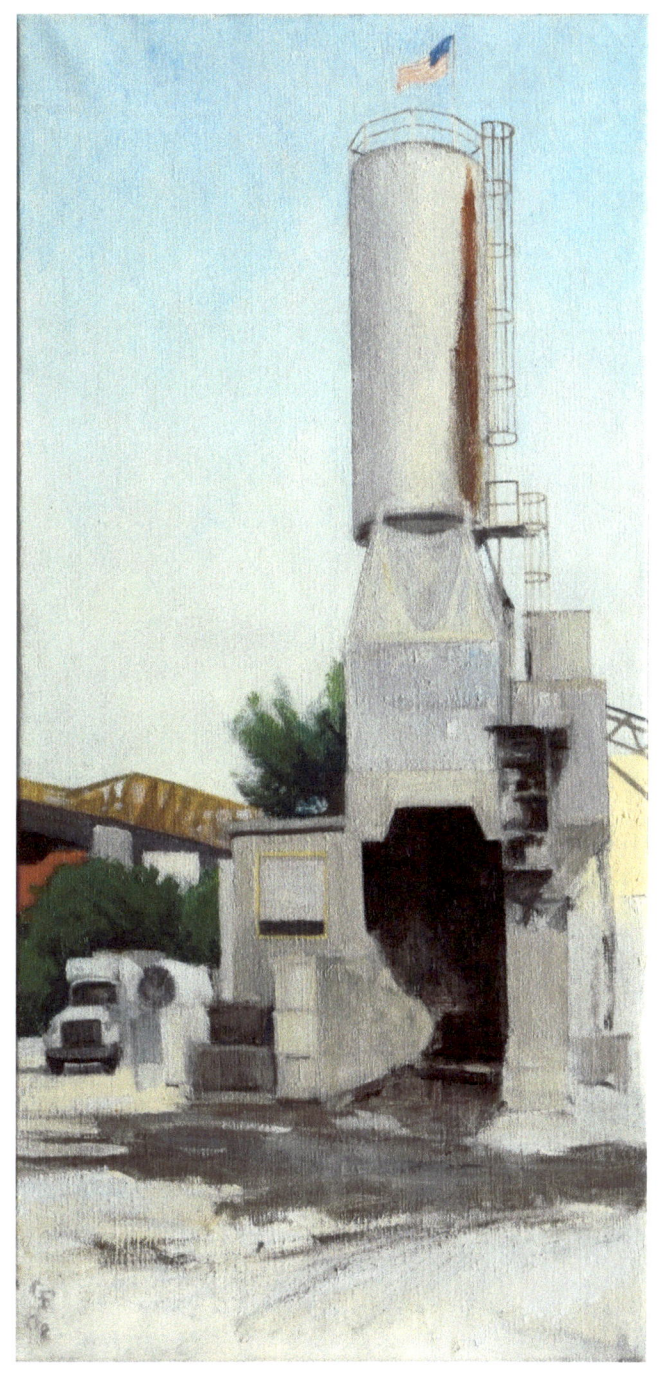

Victorian, 2003, 28" x 22" oil on canvas

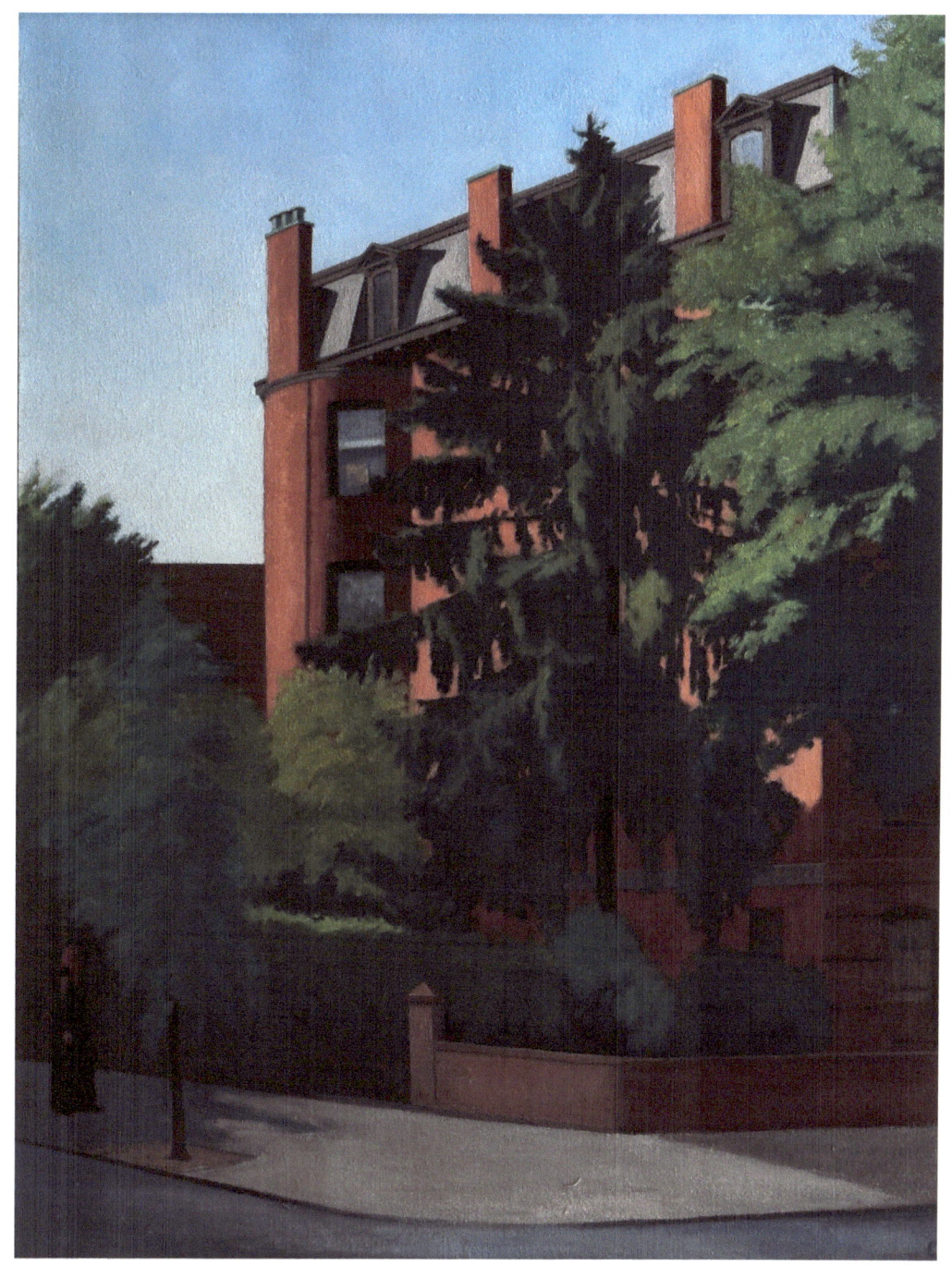

Radio (September Afternoon), 2003, 30" x 20" oil on canvas

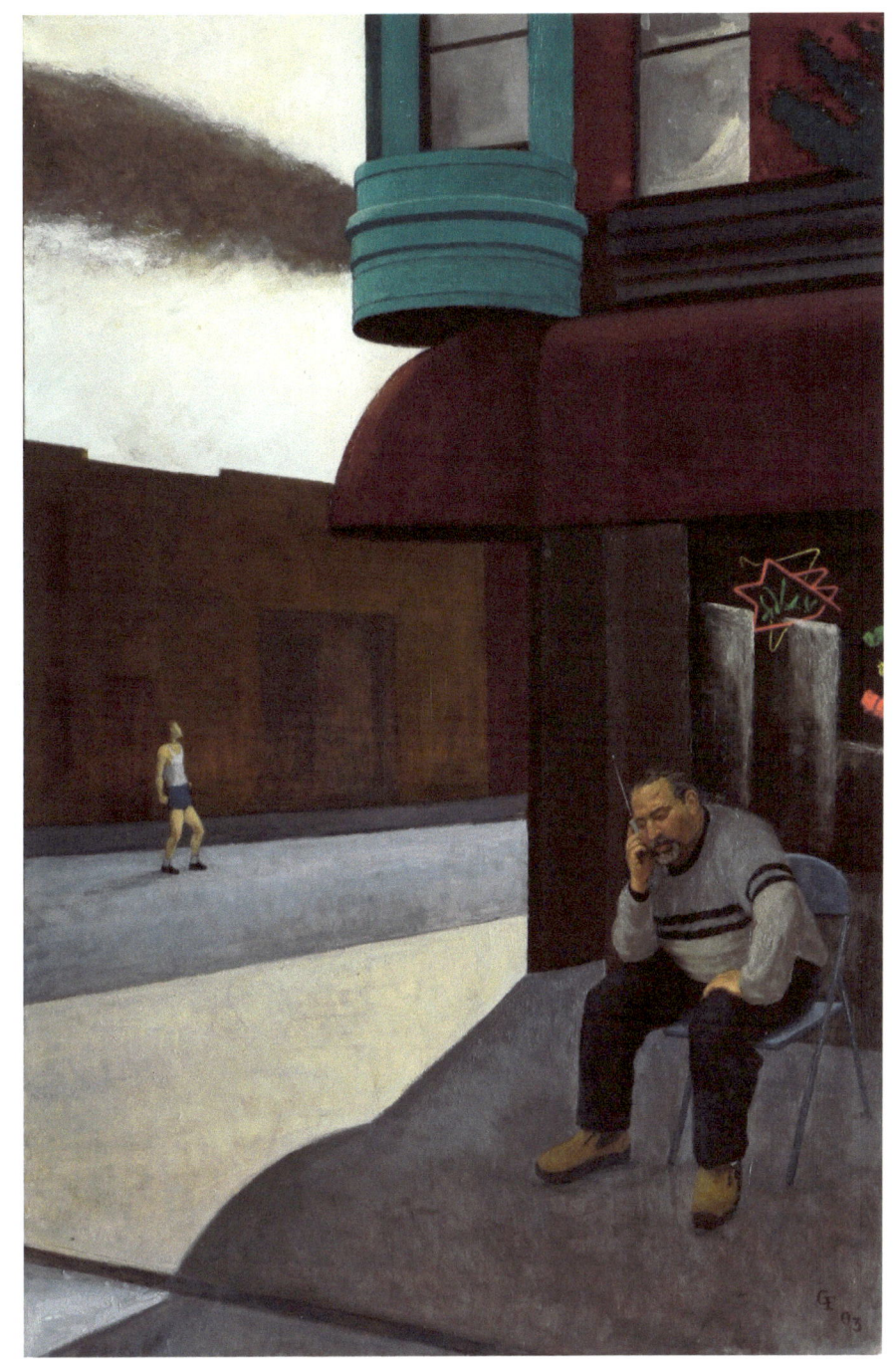

Gil's View, 2005, 24" x 18" oil on canvas

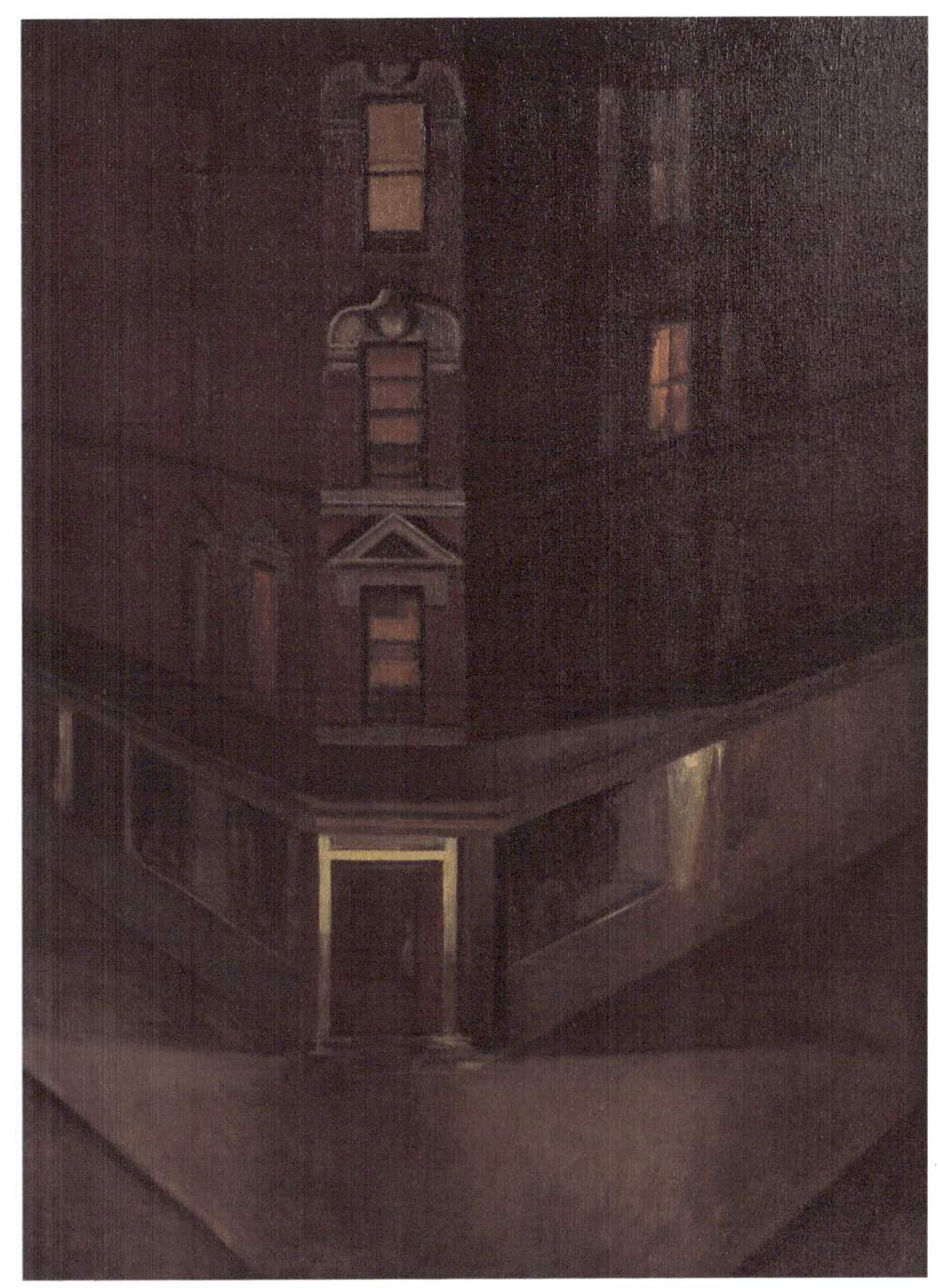

Fishing, Battery Park, 2005, 14" x 22" oil on canvas

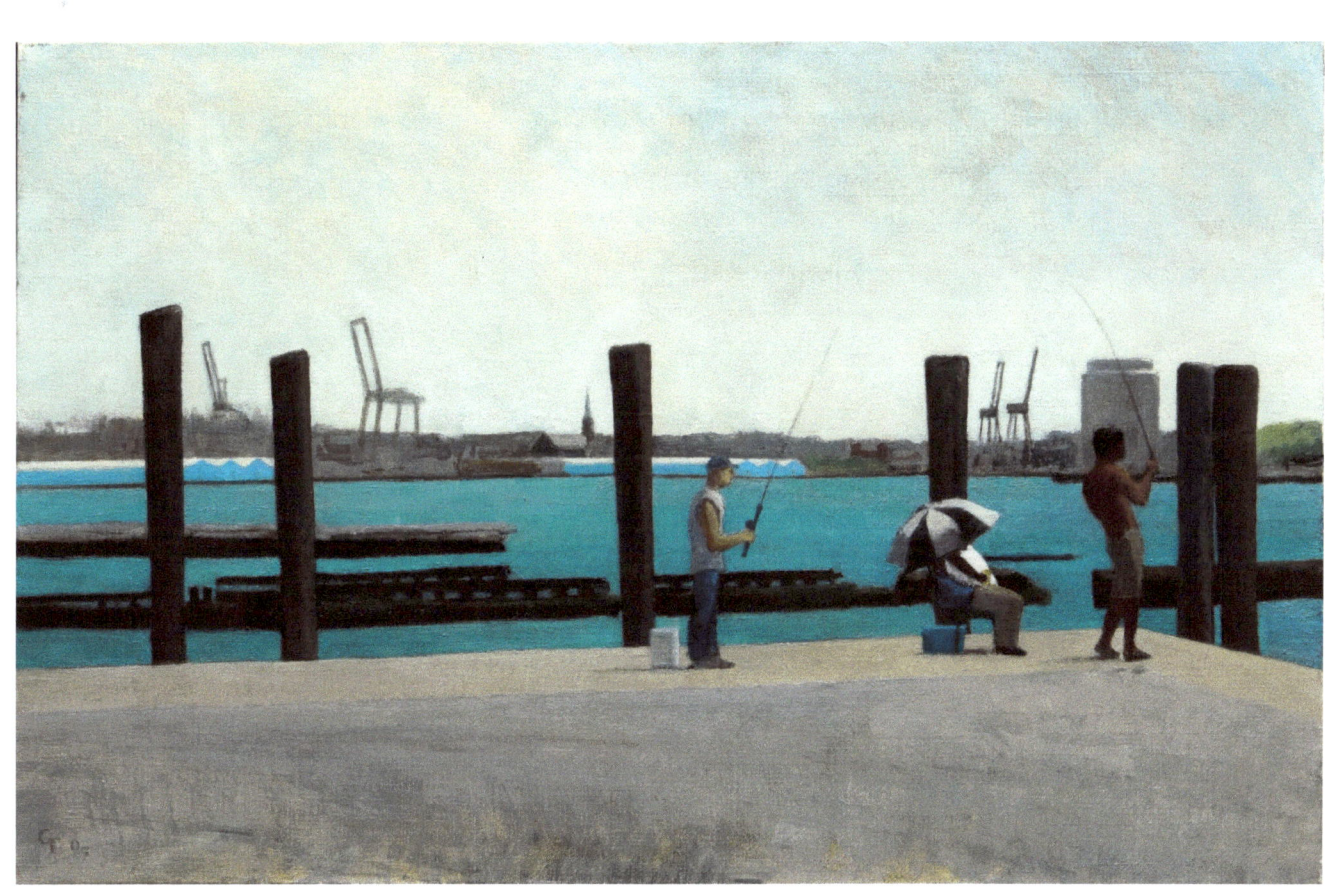

Lagoon and Bridge, 2006, 13" x 26" oil on canvas

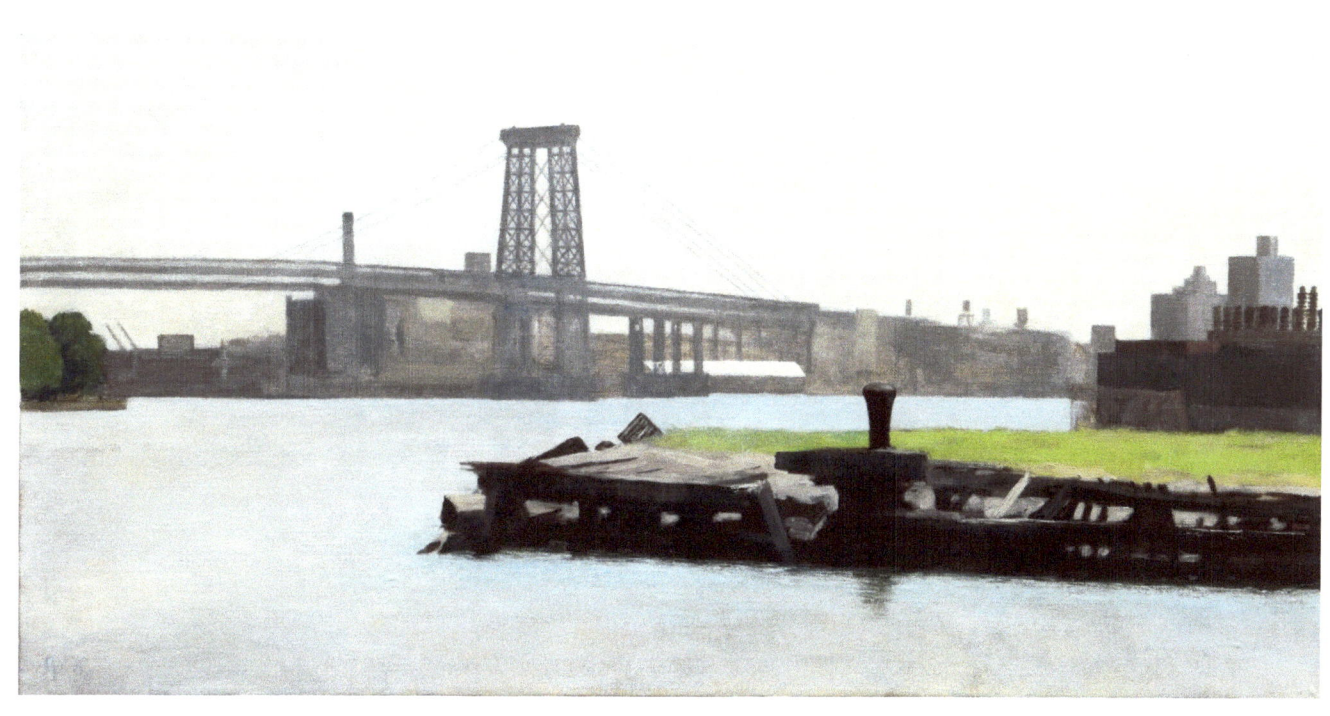

East River Kayaker, 2007, 18" x 24" oil on canvas

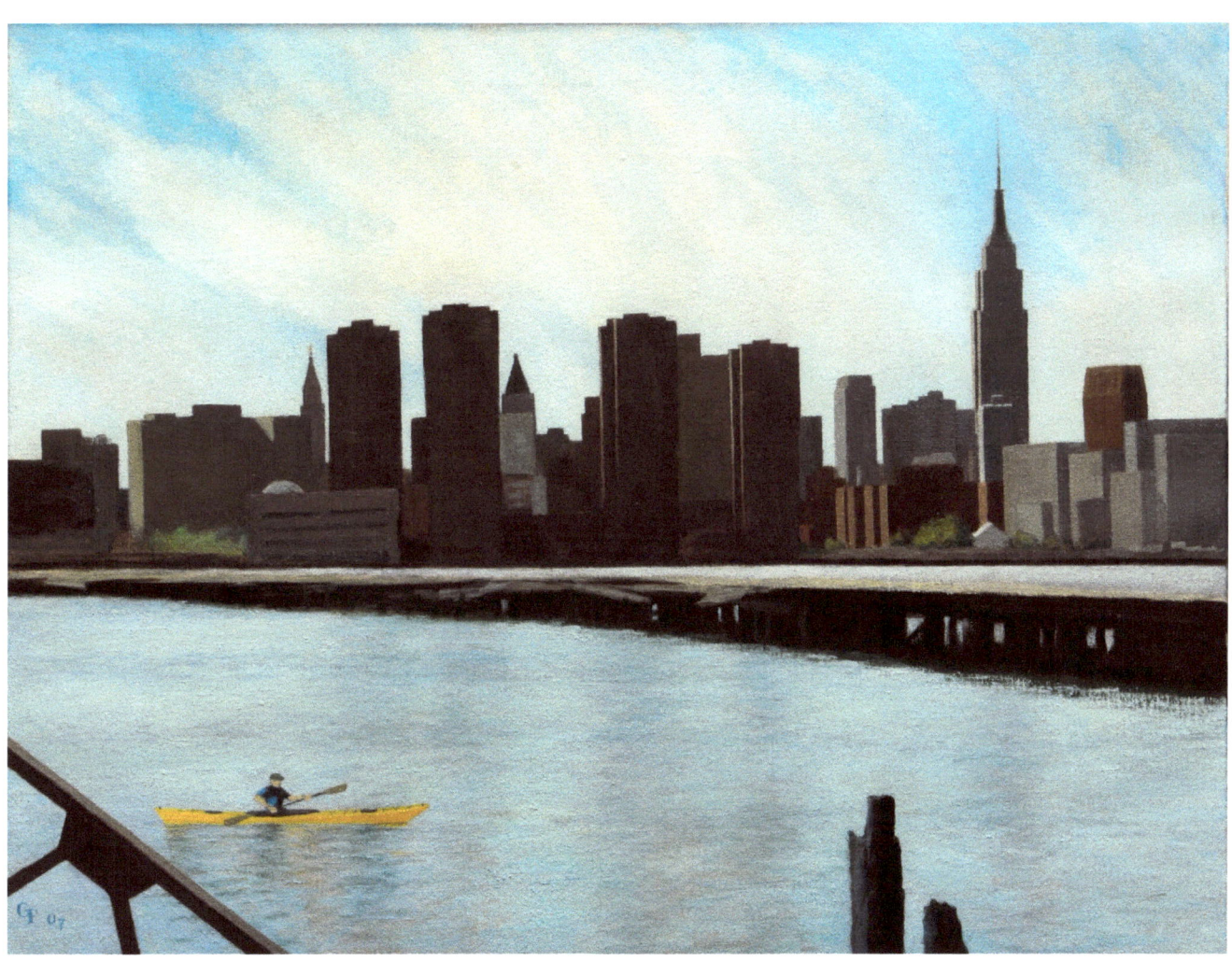

South Street for Sale, 2009, 24" x 18" oil on canvas

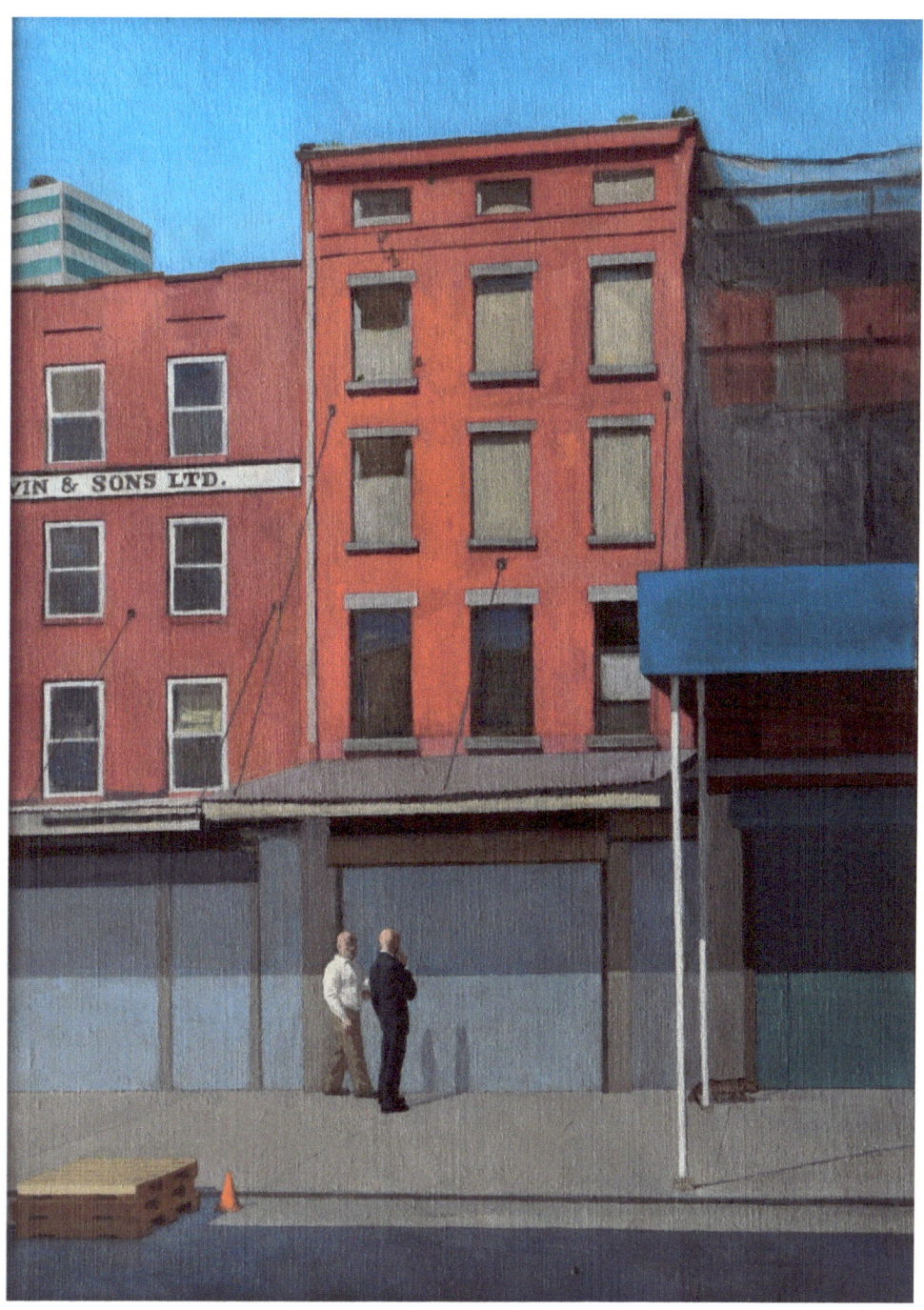

Passages, 2009, 24" x 30" oil on canvas

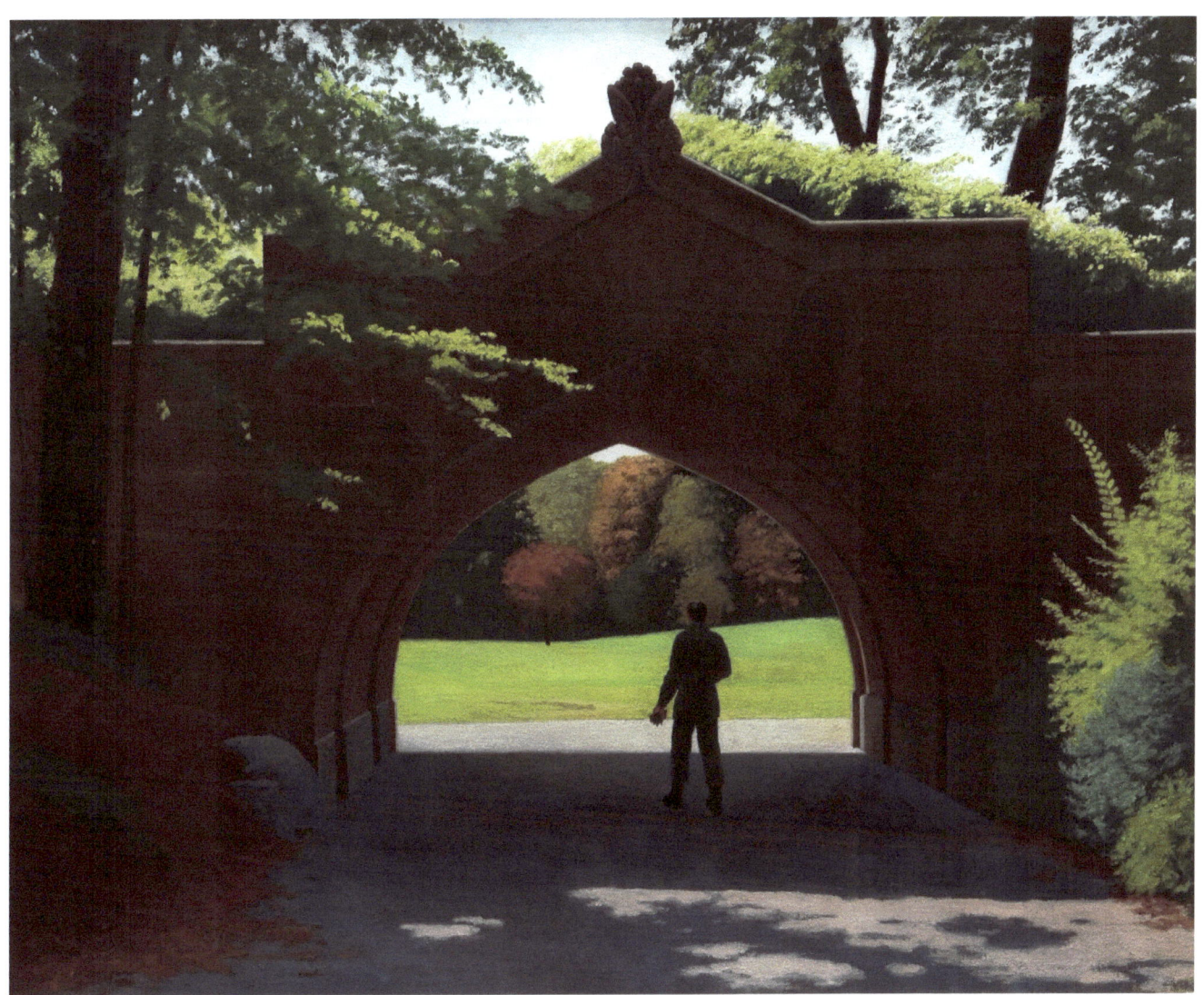

Grain Silo, 2010, 24" x 18" oil on canvas

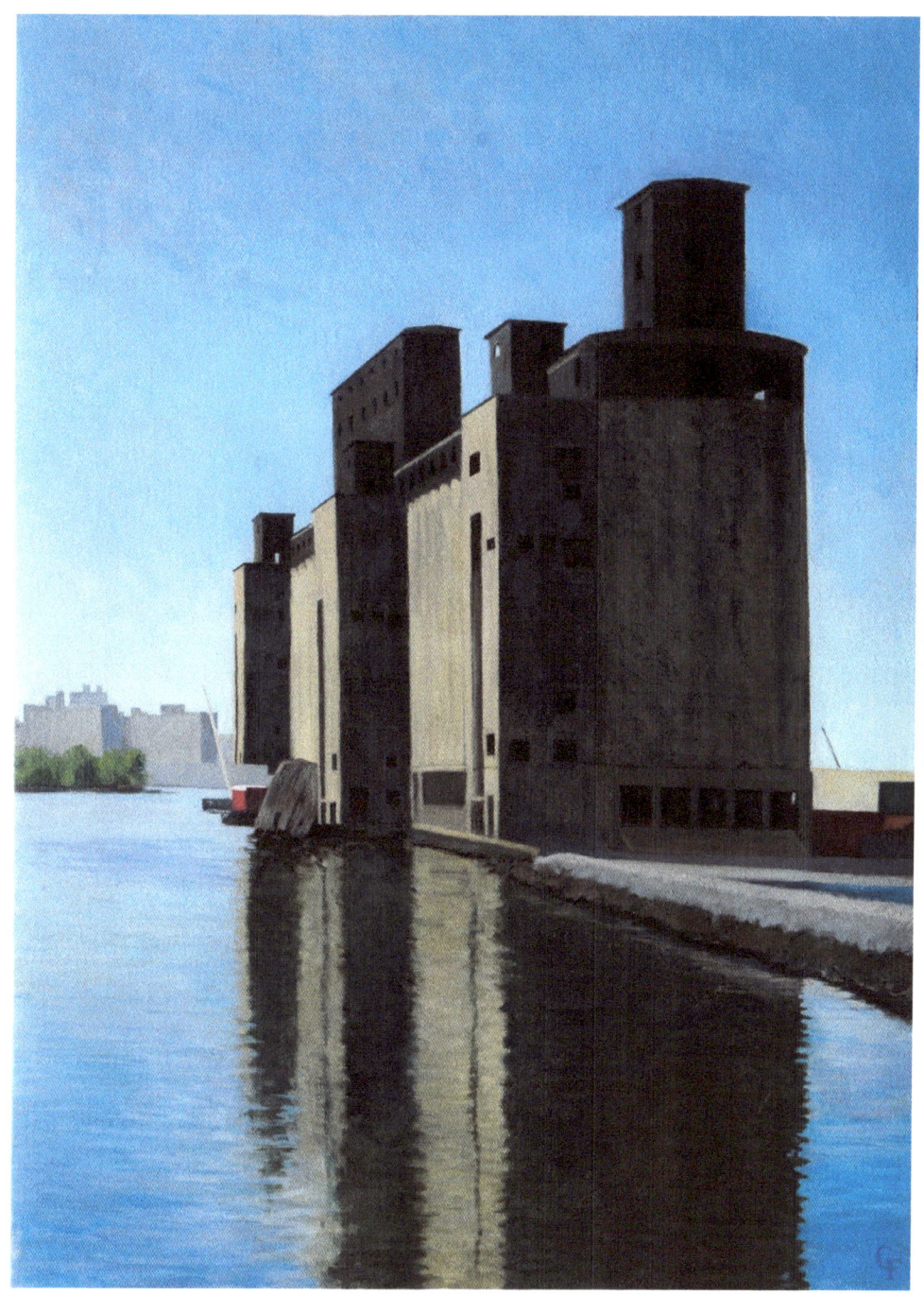

Ikea Park, 2012, 24" x 18" oil on canvas

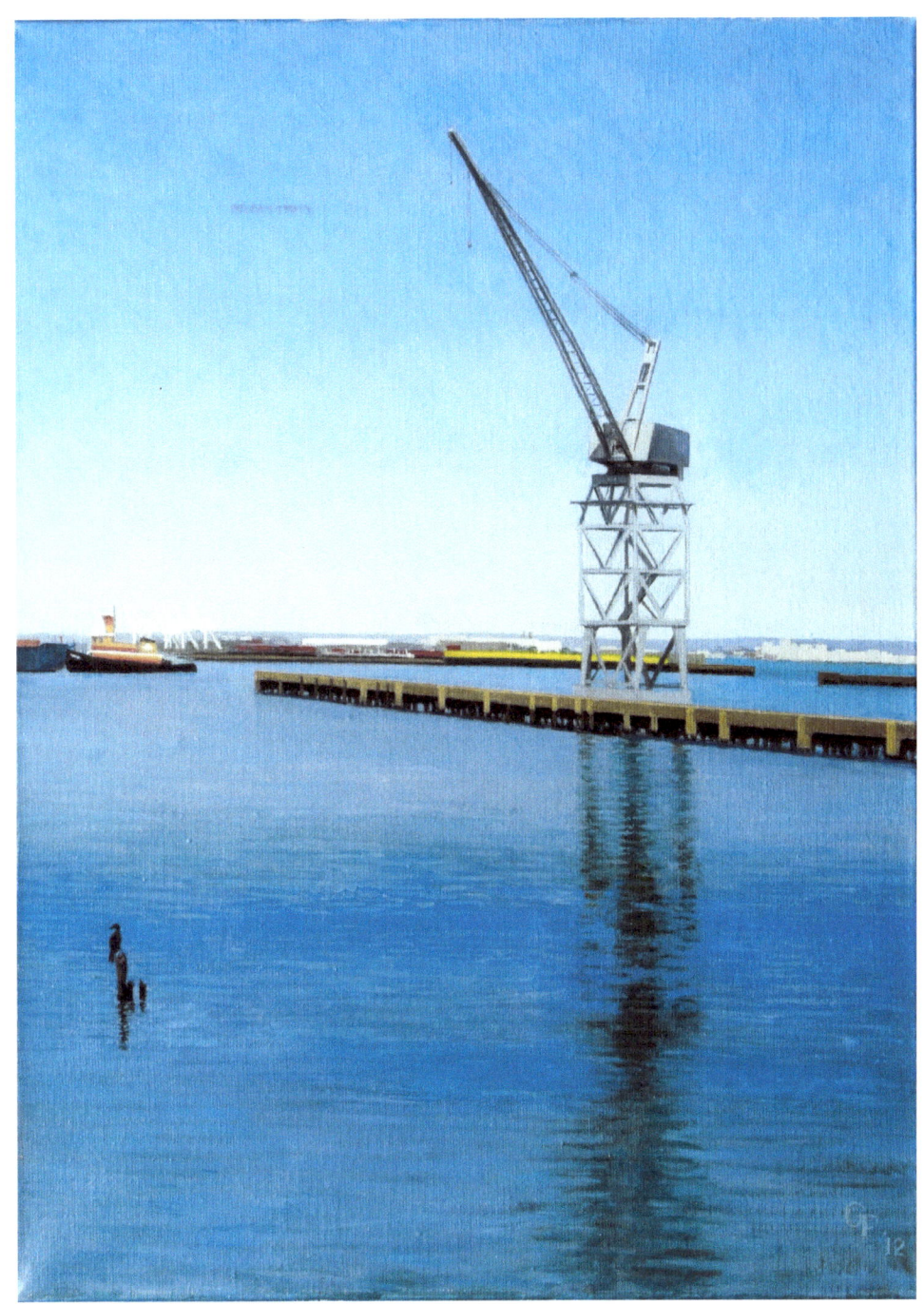

Rail Pier, 2014, 18" x 24" oil on panel

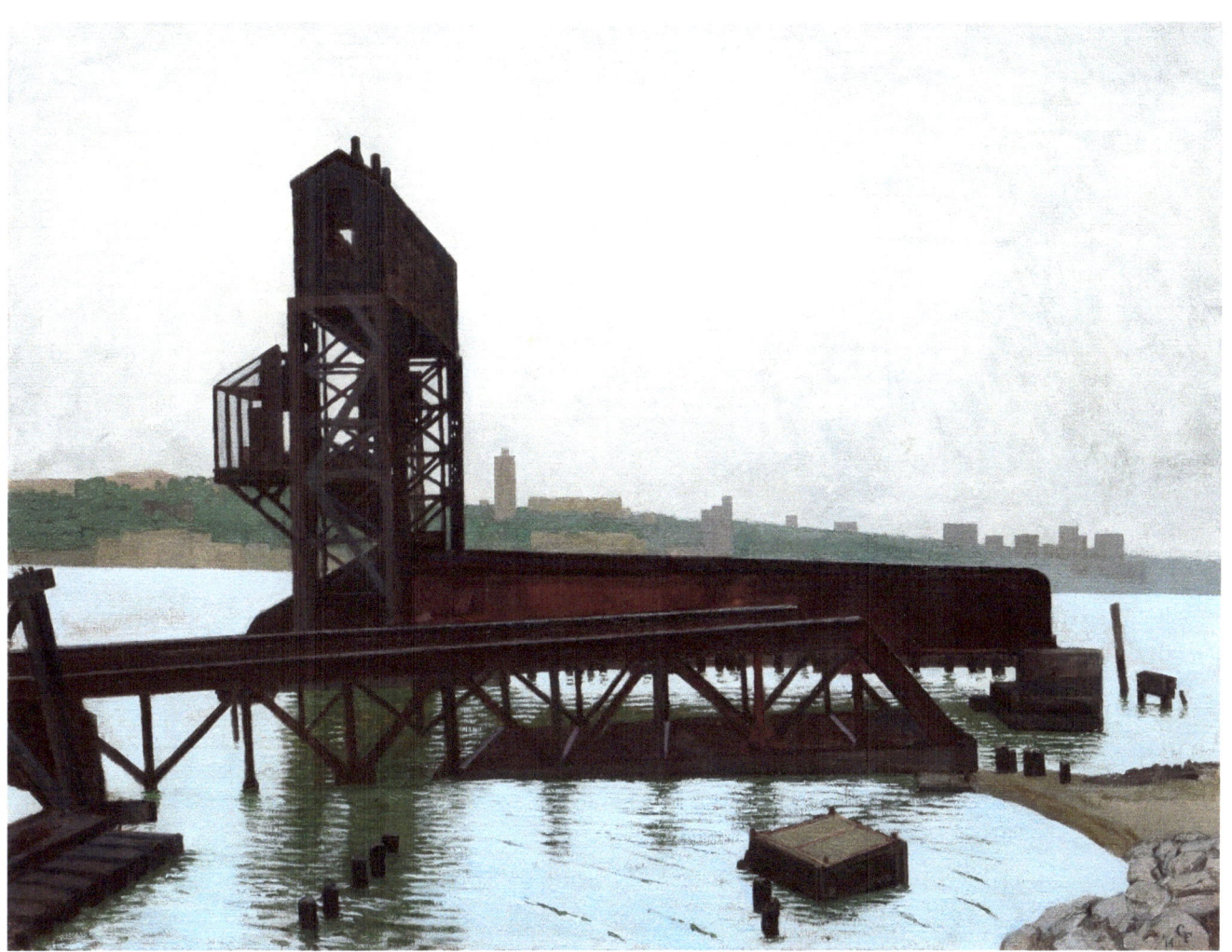

Verrazano Bridge Pier, 2014, 14" x 11" oil on panel

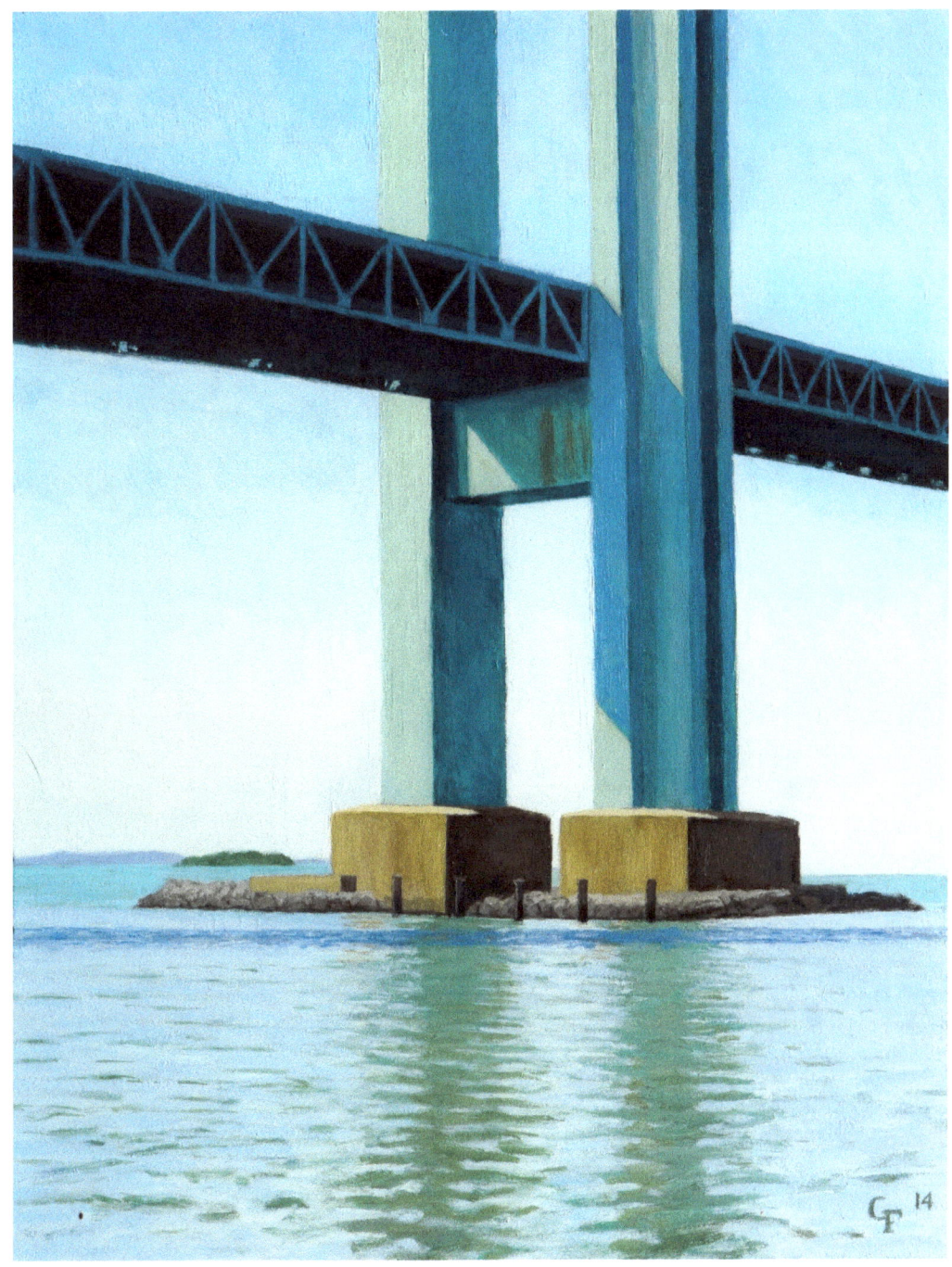

Verrazano Narrows Bridge, 2014, 18" x 24" oil on canvas

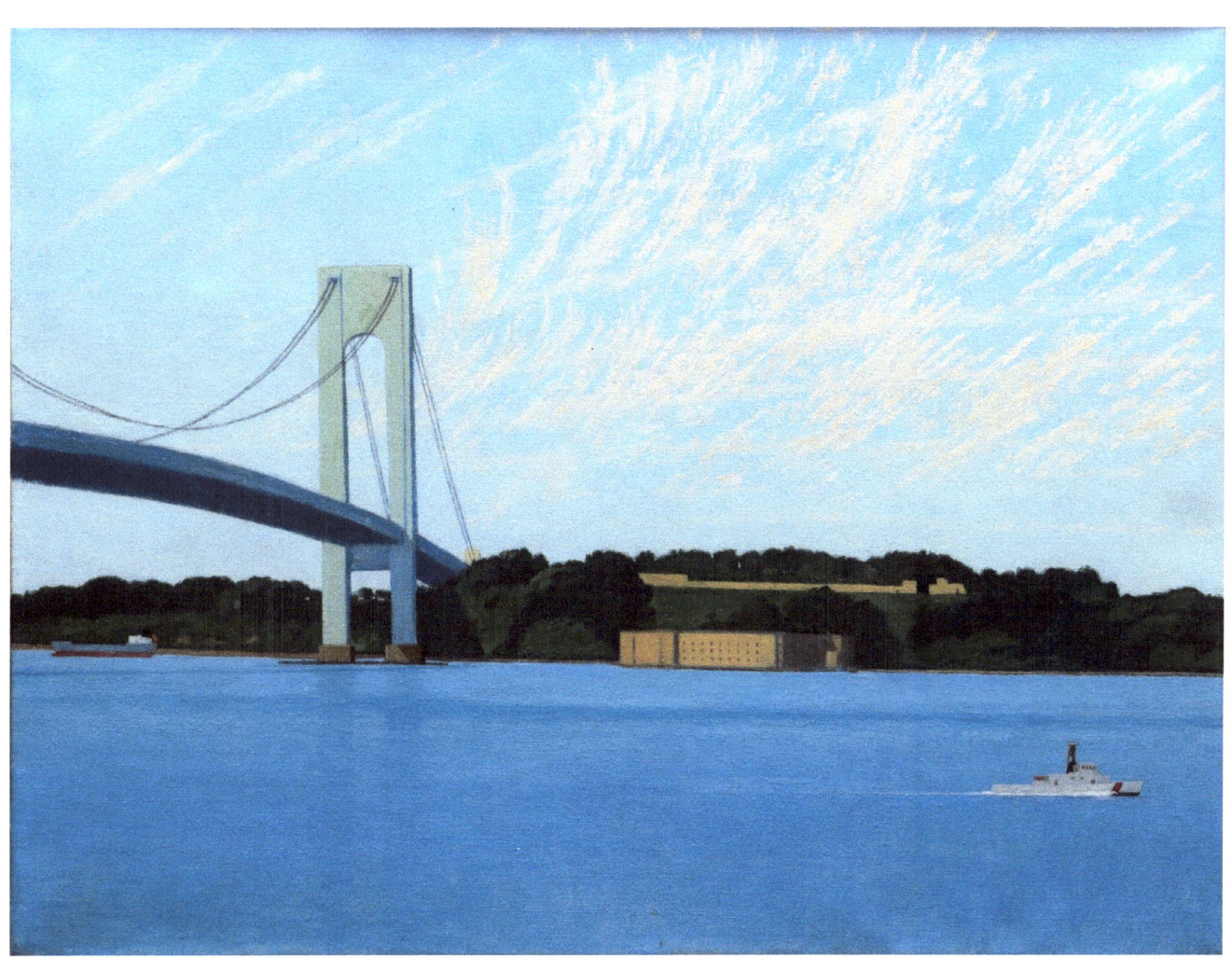

Lotus Pools, 2015, 16" x 20" oil on canvas

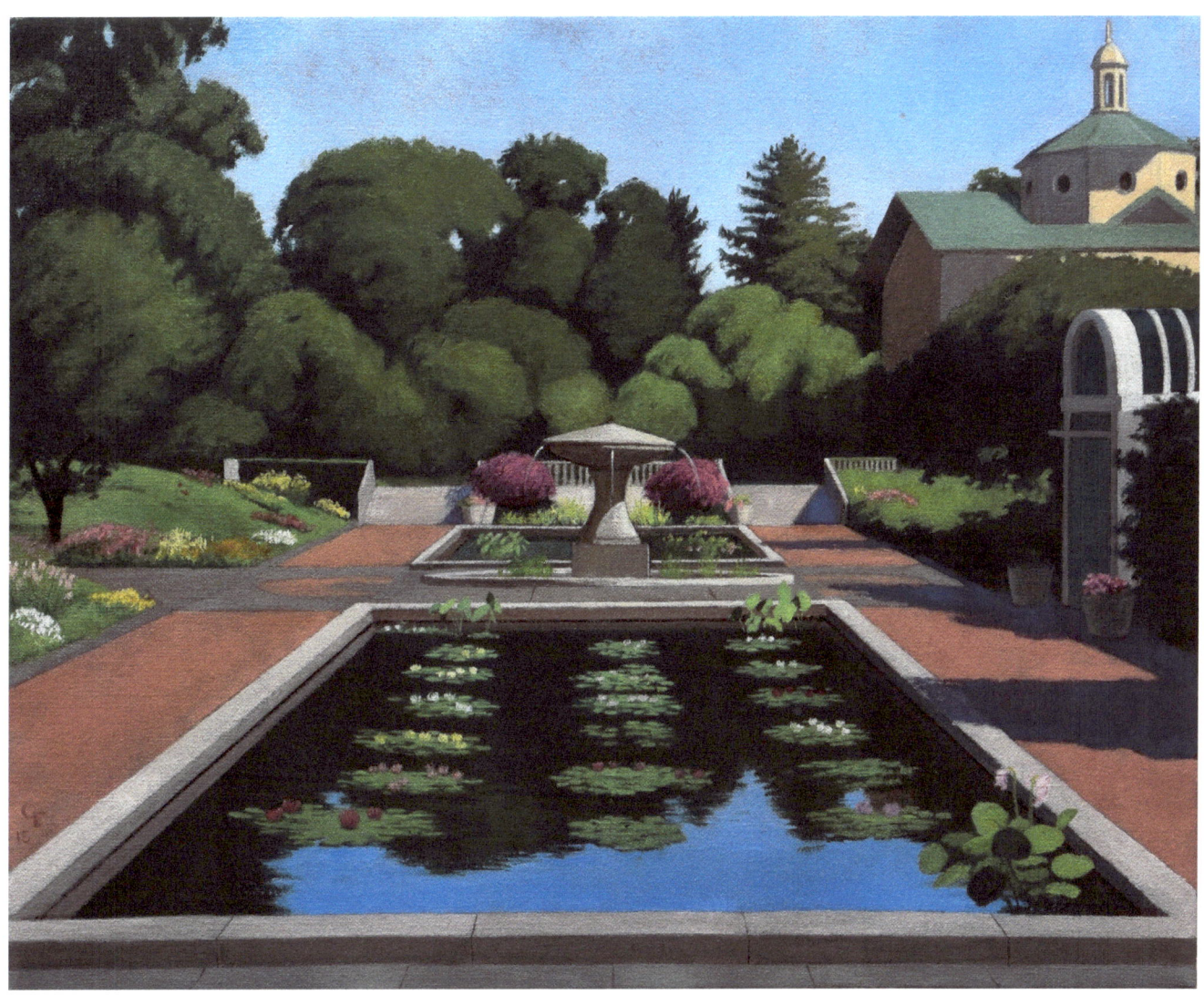

Melancholia 2, 2016, 36" x 24" oil on canvas

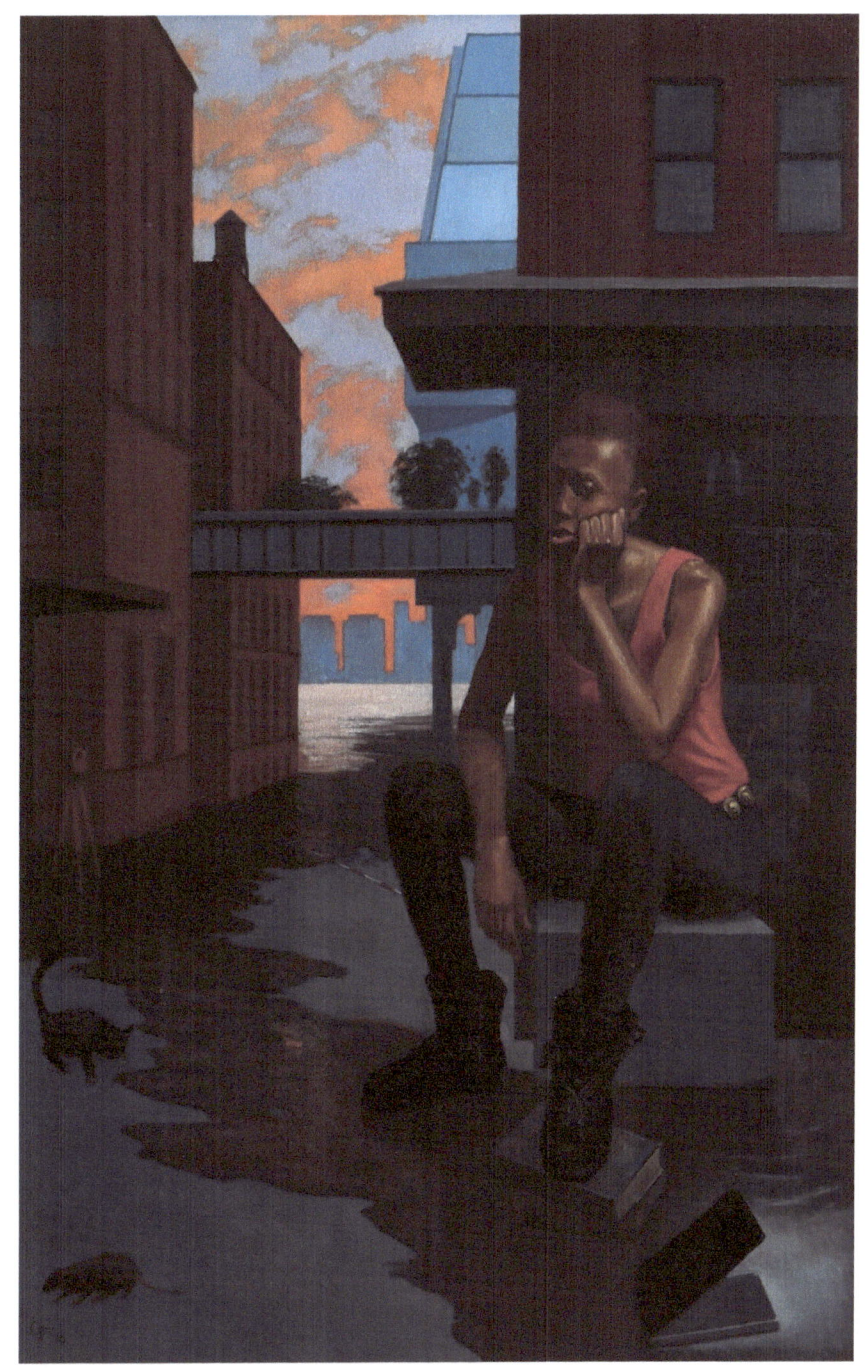

Two Arches, 2016, 24" x 30" oil on canvas

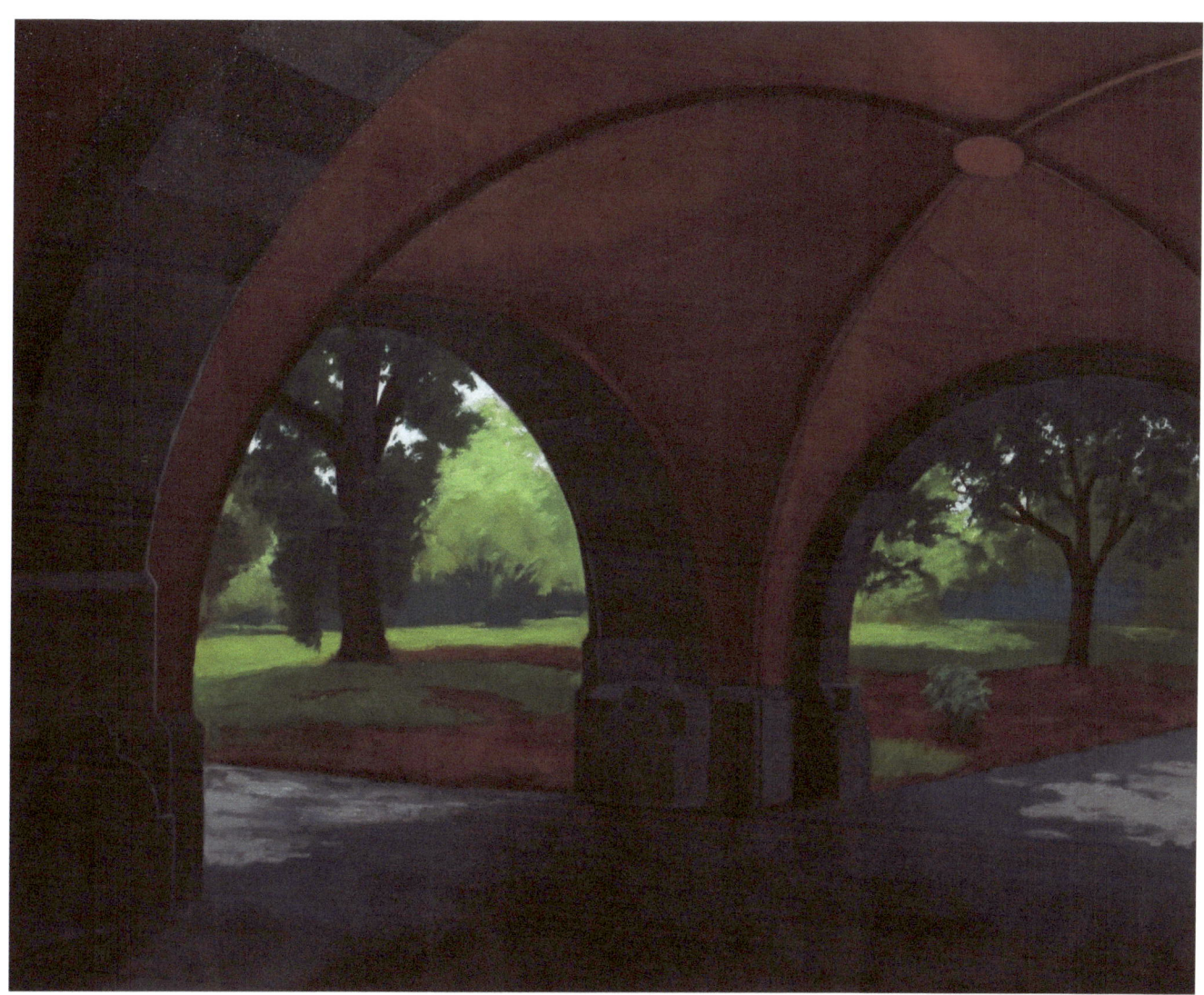

American 2017, 30" x 24" oil on canvas

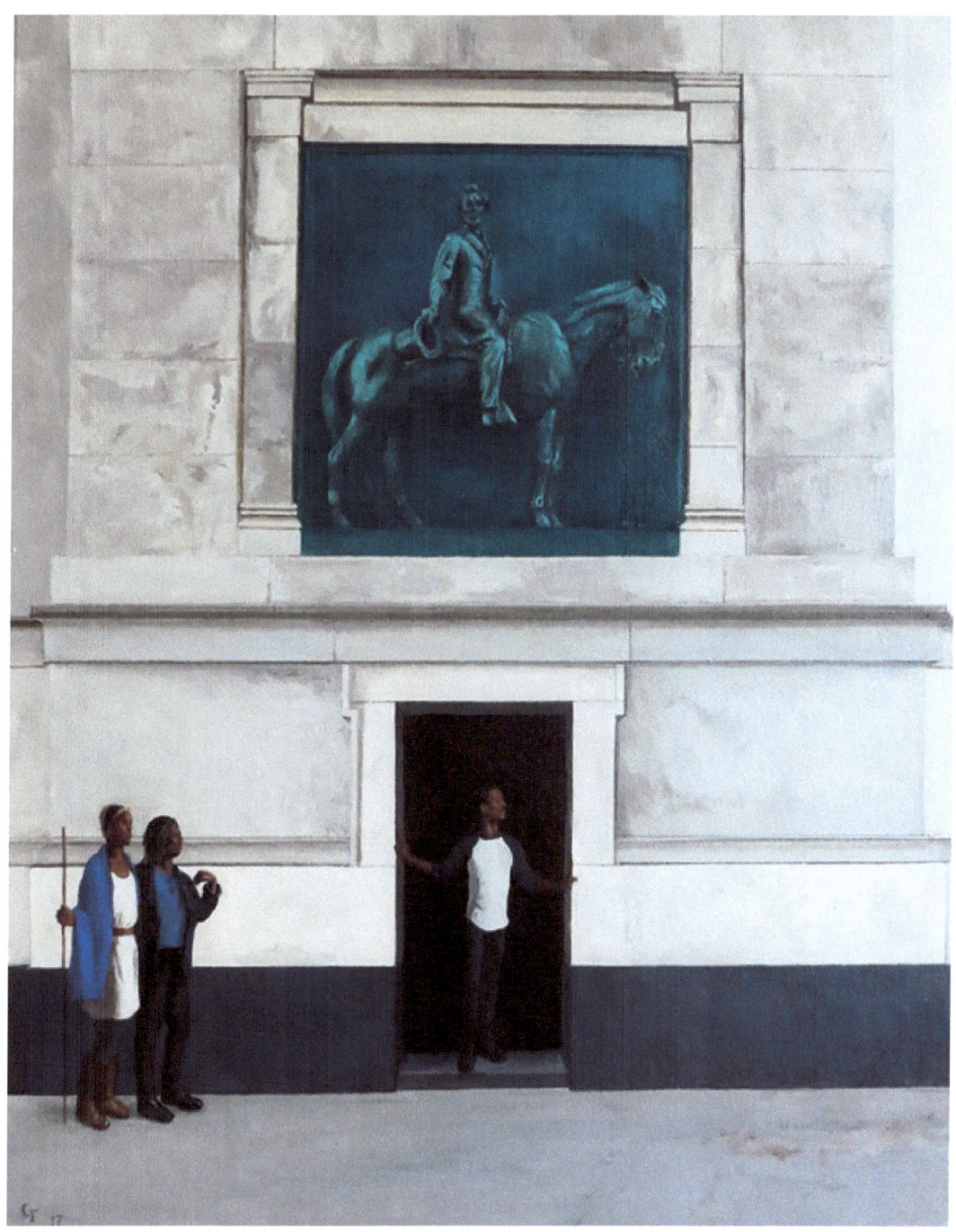

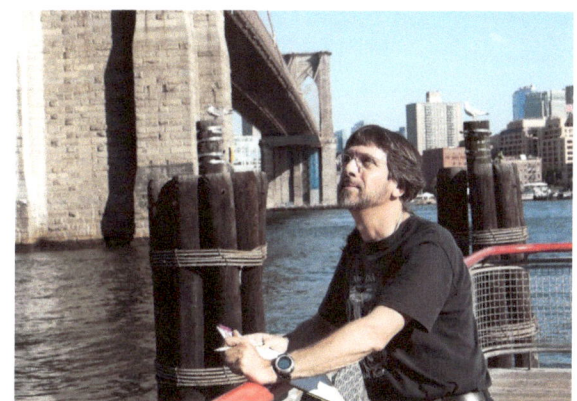
@Michele Serchuk 2016, serchukphoto.com

About Gregory Frux

Gregory Frux is a realist oil painter who finds inspiration in both urban landscapes and wilderness vistas. His cityscapes document and celebrate New York, finding beauty in unexpected places; industrial sites, bridges, brownstones, night scenes and the waterfront. The wilderness paintings are inspired by remote travel to the Rockies, Andes and Antarctica as well as the Mohave and Redrock deserts. He has served as artist in residence in four National Parks and aboard cruise ships in both Polar Regions. In 2017, he was artist in residence at the weather station at the summit of Mount Washington. His creative practice also includes illustrated travel journals, field sketching and print making. He is an occasional teacher at the Art Students League and Brooklyn Botanic Gardens. His work is in the collections of the Library of Congress, New York City Department of Education, the Metropolitan Transportation Authority, New York University, the Brooklyn Public Library and American Mountaineering Museum in Golden, Colorado.